The Girlfriend Handbook

...just for us girls

by
Laurie Newlon Hill

The Girlfriend Handbook
... just for us girls

By
Laurie Newlon Hill

Friends
Marietta, GA

FirstPublish, Inc.
Orlando, Florida

The Girlfriend Handbook
copyright 2000 by Laurie Hill

All rights reserved.
Printed and bound in the United States of America.

No part of this book covered by the copyright hereon may be reproduced in whole or in part, or used in any form or by any means—graphic, electronic, or mechanical, including photocopying, recording, taping or information storage and retrieval systems—without written permission of the publisher.

ISBN-1-929925-52-2

Illustrations by: Christina Nkirote Mugambi

FIRSTPUBLISH, INC.
170 Sunport Ln. Suite 900
Orlando, FL 32809
407-240-1414
www.firstpublish.com

Dedication

To Diane and Lisa

Table of Contents

	Page
Acknowledgments	ix
Introduction	xi
The Troupe: Girlfriends: Getting to Know Them	1
Chapter 1: Maintenance: Above & Below the Belt	15
Chapter 2: Fashion: Do's & Don'ts	31
Chapter 3: Relationships: Between the Sexes	49
Chapter 4: Diet & Exercise: Natural vs. Cosmetic	69
Chapter 5: Dating/Marriage: Should You Stay or Should You Go?	89
Chapter 6: Miscellaneous: The Junk Drawer	105

Acknowledgments

I want to express my heartfelt appreciation to all of my many girlfriends that were the very inspiration for this book. Tara, Lori, Leona (my mom), Regina (my cheerleader), Becky (my other Mom), Dona, Amy, and Sandy. They are the sisters I never had. Without their ideas, suggestions and encouragement this never would have come to print.

And I can't forget Peter who has at times been "like" a girlfriend to me and John B., my spiritual guide (he made me say that).

Introduction

While planning a birthday dinner for a girlfriend I took great pains to "do all of the right things." Frantically I hammered out the final details and preparations for the evening festivities with a fellow girlfriend. Questions flew back and forth. The following is our conversation:

"Did you make the reservations at her favorite restaurant?...Yes, done...What did you buy her?...The Mr. Microphone she has been dropping hints about for the last 6 months...Is it wrapped or in a festive bag?...Definitely wrapped and in a festive bag...Are you taking her presents in or leaving them in the car for later?...Absolutely taking them in, we want everyone to know it is her special day, don't we?...Splitting the check? ...Yes...What are you wearing?...I don't know what are you wearing?...Oh yeah, do you think we should order a cake?... Yes, of course that would be **the girlfriend thing to do!"**

The light bulb went on..."A Girlfriend Handbook" was in order! Since many standards are unwritten and are passed down from one generation to another by word of mouth it was time to put some order to these rules. The purpose of this book is to set standards of appropriate and acceptable behavior between girlfriends. The suffering, wondering, guessing and agonizing can stop when you learn "exactly what is the girlfriend thing to do". Throughout the years with friends and situations, I've discovered that no matter where you are from, what you do, or how old you are, there is proper etiquette to be followed to be a true girlfriend.

I hope that the first part of this guide will help you identify your own group— What kinds of girlfriends are out there, or even yourself. No matter what kind of girlfriend you are or choose to be, there is a common code that brings us all together. In our lives, friendships will come and go, but none will be forgotten. Come and explore the wacky world of female rituals!

The Troupe

Ms. Over Achiever

I am a realist by nature
I have a closet filled with well-tailored designer clothes
I constantly return to continuing education classes
I put my career first, second, and third
I want to own my own business, so I can be the BOSS
I am hard to reach, as I am always traveling or working late

Hobbies:
collecting frequent flyer miles
rearranging and dusting my achievement & recognition awards
balancing my 401K, IRA and stock accounts

Aspirations:
the first woman President of the United States of America

Favorite Technology:
voice mail

Ms. High Maintenance

I am very dramatic and over analytical
I am always well accessorized
I often complain about my weight without reason
I confess that cooking is not my forte
I carry everything I need in my oversized purse
I have my hair highlighted and I have my nails polished at least once a week
I am a travel nerd, but I am prepared for any emergency

Hobbies:
collecting credit cards
rearranging my cosmetic cases
renewing and indexing my fashion and entertainment magazines

Aspirations:
becoming the fashion editor for a major women's magazine
having my own cosmetic line

Favorite Technology:
16-way makeup mirror

Ms. Social Coordinator

I supply the "girlfriend glue" to my circle of friends
I have an annoyingly positive attitude
I like to be the center of attention by cracking jokes
I can't miss a phone call
I remember all special occasions

Hobbies:
perfecting call-waiting techniques
visiting greeting card stores
listening to "oldies" on the radio station

Aspirations:
becoming a lounge singer or a professional party planner

Favorite Technology:
cordless telephone

Ms. Politically Correct
I must be outdoors at least 23 hours a day
I don't use plastic or aerosol cans
I am a vegetarian
I am very competitive
I like to exercise every day

Hobbies:
recycling
coordinating protests
hugging trees

Aspirations:
to save the planet

Favorite Technology:
none

Ms. Melodrama

I am always desperately seeking a man even though I say I don't need one
I try all the latest diet fads
I am hooked on self-help books that my therapist recommends
I often think about moving to "start over", life is surely happening if I am not there
I believe the glass is not only half – empty, but it also needs to be washed

Hobbies:
attending therapy
answering personal ads
collecting gym membership cards
counting fat grams
reciting affirmations

Aspirations:
having my own talk show focusing on finding one's inner self

Favorite Technology:
electronic scales

Ms. Fix-It

I don't like any one to fight, but I will if I have to
I am the "Mother Hen" of the group, even when I was 12 years old
I belong to at least 20 committees
I am handy with a thread, needle and a glue gun
I have always strived to be the "good" daughter, sister and friend
I make all of my own curtains and holiday decorations

Hobbies:
attending craft fairs
perfecting hugging techniques
cultivating my herb and vegetable garden

Aspirations:
writing my own combination craft and cookbook

Favorite Technology:
any cordless tool

Chapter 1

Maintenance
above & below the belt

A Good Girlfriend...

Not only compliments, but also remembers your good hair days. Even if it was two years ago.

A Good Girlfriend...

Assures you that the new skin regimen definitely makes you look 6 months younger than you really are.

A Good Girlfriend...

Helps you in your rationalization for all of your hair product purchases, especially the STATE OF THE ART- MEGA TURBO-TO DIE FOR-CAN'T LIVE WITHOUT- VOLUMIZING- HIGH-TECH HAIR DRYER
... for the ultimate hair day.

A Good Girlfriend...

Subtly hints when an obsessive behavior is taking over your life.

A Good Girlfriend...

Suggests the "Wonder Bra" over implant surgery.

A Good Girlfriend...

Confirms that it's not even noticeable.

A Good Girlfriend...

Informs you that HIGH MAINTENANCE is not a term for a pricey mechanic.

A Good Girlfriend...

Knows and accepts you when you are HIGH-MAINTENANCE.

A test to see if you fit into this category:
__Do you need 4 styling brushes for your hair?
__Do you take 3 of your own pillows on a one-day trip?
__Do you need a tackle box to accommodate all of your makeup?
__Do you need 6 alarm clocks to get you up in the morning and you are still late for work?
__Do you buy your cosmetics in bulk?
__Do you have your own home repair kit to fix your broken nails?
__Is your purse bigger than your grandmother's?
__Do you coordinate your outfits to match your cell phones and pagers?

If you answered yes to any of these questions, then you are a high maintenance girlfriend.

A Good Girlfriend...

Is there when you discover your first gray hair, your first wrinkle and your first spider vein.

# A Good Girlfriend...

Will meet you at the hair salon so you can spend time together.

"Old Friends"

We meet so many pleasant folks
as we walk this world through,
"Old friends" might think they're forgotten
While you're busy with the new.

But I've found this true a thousand times
and I've put it to the test,
When you really, really need a friend
"old friends" are the best.

By...Dolores Bain Patterson

Chapter 2

Fashion
do's & don'ts

A Good Girlfriend...

Pledges on the "Girlfriend Handbook", that 100% spandex outfits WILL go out of style.

A Good Girlfriend...

Extends an open invitation to her closet, and doesn't care if you pick something that still has the tag on it.

A Good Girlfriend...

Keeps you abreast of all sales and as an added plus provides you with a strategic map so you can optimize your shopping experience.

A Good Girlfriend...

Keeps you informed of fashion "do's and don'ts."

A Good Girlfriend...

Is always on duty as the "Fashion Police" and will arrest you if necessary.

A Good Girlfriend...

Tries to comprehend all of your "fashion" phases and prays that they are truly phases.

A Good Girlfriend...

Never buys you the annual Sports Illustrated Swimsuit edition when the much dreaded bathing suit season approaches.

A Good Girlfriend...

Will let you know if you have VPL (visible panty lines).

A Good Girlfriend...

Is honest with you when you ask, "Does this make me look fat?"

 **A Good Girlfriend...**

Never buys you clothes with horizontal stripes.

A Good Girlfriend...

Agrees to the fact that some sadistic person invented completely different mirrors for the fitting rooms.

A Good Girlfriend...

Notifies you if you are wearing white out of "season".

A Good Girlfriend...

Does not insist that the bridesmaid dress you had to purchase for her wedding can easily be transformed to an evening gown. She knows that is never going to happen.

Chapter 3

Relationships
between the sexes

A Good Girlfriend...

Is the voice of encouragement.

A Good Girlfriend...

Reminds you that it is HIS loss!

A Good Girlfriend...

Is there to remind you that HE is never going to change.

A Good Girlfriend...

Is your mom, or maybe not.

A Good Girlfriend...

Is there to pick up the pieces.

 A Good Girlfriend...

Never underestimates the power of PMS.

A Good Girlfriend...

Pretends to like HIM, if he makes you happy.

# A Good Girlfriend…

Backs all of your career aspirations, (even if it is a lounge singer).

A Good Girlfriend...

Vows to help you find yourself and feels your pain.

A Good Girlfriend...

Is only a phone call, or two, or three away.

A Good Girlfriend...

Ponders with you the ever-elusive question: "Why can't men treat and understand us like our girlfriends"?

A Good Girlfriend...

Realizes that not all news can wait.

A Good Girlfriend...

Shares the remote control.

A Good Girlfriend...

Doesn't care if you are always "politically correct".

A Good Girlfriend...

Helps you prepare for your class reunion.

A Good Girlfriend…

Will procrastinate with you.

A Good Girlfriend...

Is there to build a lifetime of memories.

Chapter 4

Diet & Exercise
natural vs. cosmetic

# A Good Girlfriend...

Will do whatever it takes to get you into your favorite pair of jeans.

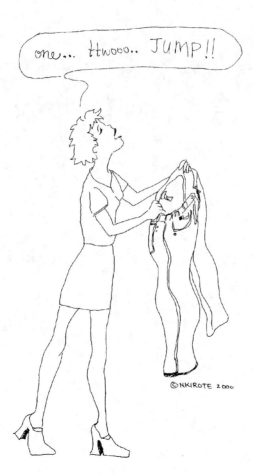

A Good Girlfriend...

Would never buy you a bathroom scale for a present.

A Good Girlfriend...

Doesn't let you become a slave to the "Thigh Master™" or the "Stair Master™".

A Good Girlfriend...

Forbids you to use the vacuum as a way to cut costs on liposuction surgery.

A Good Girlfriend...

Agrees that you should start your diet on Monday.

A Good Girlfriend...

Assures you that skinny people have cellulite, too!

A Good Girlfriend...

Doesn't question when you order a diet coke and at the same time you order a quadruple fudge cake with chocolate ice cream for dessert.

A Good Girlfriend...

Tells you that your stomach looks bigger to you because you are looking down on it.

 A Good Girlfriend...

Knows that diet is a four-letter word.

A Good Girlfriend...

Would never tell anyone that you had an intake of 300 fat grams in one sitting.

A Good Girlfriend...

Does not accept a bribe so you will work out with her.

A Good Girlfriend...

Agrees that the scales at the doctor's office are set five pounds heavier.

A Good Girlfriend...

Will try the latest diet craze with you.

Growing up together sharing
Intimate wants and desires
Respecting individuality along the way
Laughing and crying
Forgiving beyond all boundaries
Reminiscing over past moments of
Insanity
Exiting in and out of our lives
Never forgetting our bonds as
Dear
Sisters and confidants   By Laurie Newlon Hill

Chapter 5

Dating/Marriage
should you stay or should you go?

A Good Girlfriend...

Will listen for the umpteenth time as you gush on about the newest man in your life.

..... Hello...
..... Hey girl? How are you? Good! I'm fine, actually I'm great!! Did I tell you about Rick? I did, well, you won't believe what he did yesterday.... We were out at Navori's in Bankhead and I was wearing that new dress, you know, the little black and silver one that I saved all month for, anyway, he takes one look at me and says "Oh ma gosh, you look soo next millenium!! I have never gone out with anyone so trendy before!" And THEN, he excused himself from the table, went to Racha's and bought himself a new suit... it was black and silver too!! Can you believe it?! THEN, after dinner we drove down to the docks, the moon was out, and so were the stray cats.... but that was alright because it was sooo romantic and I knew that he is it!!

A Good Girlfriend...

Knows it is her duty to remember every detail of her date, especially if it is the FIRST date.

A Good Girlfriend...

Assures you HE will call.

# A Good Girlfriend...

Does not discourage you if you want to take a class in Knife Throwing, because you could meet Mr. Wonderful there.

A Good Girlfriend...

Is there to bail you out of a blind date, if necessary.

A Good Girlfriend...

Lets you borrow her tape of all your favorite television shows that you missed because you finally had a DATE!

# A Good Girlfriend...

Doesn't let you get lost on the information highway.

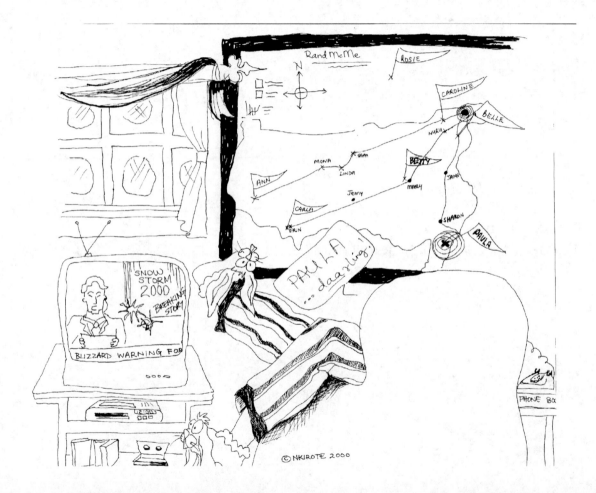

A Good Girlfriend...

Has a spare room, especially if she lives in a strategic location that will provide cheap, yet prime vacation spots.

A Good Girlfriend...

Mans the fire extinguisher when you have the ceremonial burning of all the photographs of your ex-boyfriends, ex-husbands, or ex-whatevers.

A Good Girlfriend...

Realizes that even if you are married/divorced/single… you still need a G.N.O. (Girl's Night Out).

Chapter 6

Miscellaneous
the junk drawer

A Good Girlfriend...

Never criticizes if you are singing out of tune or blaring out the wrong words to a song.

A Good Girlfriend...

Never dates one of your ex-boyfriends, ex-husbands or ex-whatevers.

A Good Girlfriend...

Will wire and program your VCR, personal computer, pager, or cell phone.

A Good Girlfriend...

Accompanies you in all drive-bys: a drive-by his house, a drive-by his office, or a drive-by his hangouts.

A Good Girlfriend...

Lets you drive her new car and does not worry about your past driving history.

A Good Girlfriend...

Shares with you her helpful cooking tips, straight from the Girlfriend Kitchen:

1. Ultimate Lean Cuisine™ - microwave on high for 6.5 minutes. Remove and chow down.
2. Scrumptious and Wild Weight Watchers™ - microwave on high for 3.5 minutes. Rotate and remove plastic film cover and heat for an additional 1.5 minutes on low setting.
3. Luscious Lip Smacking Budget Gourmet™ - microwave on high for 4 minutes. Lift corner of carton and cook an additional 2 minutes. Let stand for 1 minute to ensure thorough cooking.

NOTE: all desserts will compliment any of the above, the choice is up to the cook. Bon Appetite!

# A Good Girlfriend...

Helps you balance your checkbook.

A Good Girlfriend...

Refuses to encourage you to call the "psychic hot line" for advice.

A Good Girlfriend...

Has call waiting.

A Good Girlfriend...

Will stop and get directions.

Do you have some rules you would like to share?

We need help for volume II of the Girlfriend Handbook. Please share with us any rules that we did not mention, but you know within your friendships. Go to www.thegirlfriendhandbook.com and post your rules.

If your local bookstore is out of stock, copies may be obtained by going to our website www.thegirlfriendhandbook.com, or to www.firstpublish.com.

Books are available at special discounts when purchased in bulk for premiums and sales promotions as well as for fund raising or educational use. Special editions or excerpts can also be created to specification. For details, contact Customer Service at the address below.

FirstPublish, Inc.
170 Sunport Lane
Suite #900
Orlando, FL 32809
888-707-7634